Travel Journal

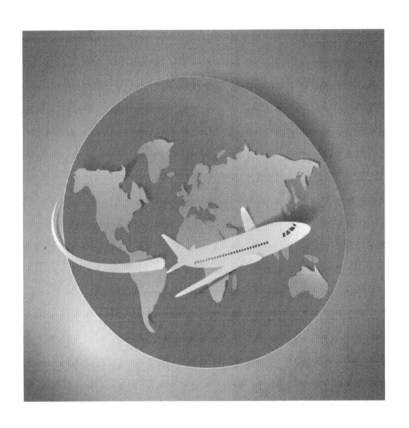

The Publisher: Wandering Walks of Wonder Publishing

Kansas City, MO 64118

USA

Website: www.wanderingwalksofwonder.com

ISBN-13: 978-1515018421

ISBN-10: 1515018423

This Journal

Belongs to:

_____

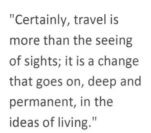

"Certainly, travel is
more than the seeing
of sights; it is a change
that goes on, deep and
permanent, in the
ideas of living."

~Mary Ritter Beard

Travel is a time for growth, new experiences, and seeing more of the world. If you're going on a trip, you'll want to remember everything you did. A travel journal will enrich your trip at the time and will preserve your memories of the experience.

How to write a Travel Journal

If you are going to write a travel journal:
• Make sure this journal and pen are on your packing list.
• Decide who you are writing this journal for. Our travel journals are written for us. Sometimes they contain witty prose and humor and sometimes they just contains facts we want to remember.. I would also suggest you write for yourself.
• Jot down notes every day that will help you remember the details of the day. If you don't have time to write a journal entry, just keep a list of your notes in the back of whatever you are using for a journal.
• Set aside time in the evening, at breakfast, on plane, train or car rides to take these facts and write your journal entries. Try and write something for every day of your trip.

Suggestions

• Think about what you saw that surprised you.
• Think about what amused you.
• Think about the sights, smells, tastes, and sounds.
• What was the name of that guide, site, etc?
• Take a picture of that historic plaque to help you with details you may want later.
• Don't worry too much about editing, spelling or grammar. This journal is for you. You can clean it up later.

Date:	Starting From:	Companions
	Destination:	
Weather:	Towns and Cities Explored:	Towns and Cities Explored:

Today's Travel Reflections:

Sites Visited:

_____

_____

_____

_____

_____

_____

_____

_____

_____

_____

I Will Never Forget:

_____

_____

_____

_____

_____

_____

_____

_____

_____

Date:	Starting From:	Companions
	Destination:	
Weather: ☀ ⛅ 🌧 🌨	Towns and Cities Explored:	Towns and Cities Explored:

Today's Travel Reflections:

_____

_____

_____

_____

_____

_____

_____

_____

_____

_____

_____

_____

_____

_____

_____

_____

_____

_____

Sites Visited:

_____

_____

_____

_____

_____

_____

_____

_____

_____

_____

I Will Never Forget:

_____

_____

_____

_____

_____

_____

_____

_____

_____

_____

Date:	Starting From:	Companions
	Destination:	
Weather: ☀ ⛅ 🌧 🌨	Towns and Cities Explored:	Towns and Cities Explored:

Today's Travel Reflections:

_____

_____

_____

_____

_____

_____

_____

_____

_____

_____

_____

_____

_____

_____

_____

_____

_____

Sites Visited:

_____

_____

_____

_____

_____

_____

_____

_____

_____

_____

I Will Never Forget:

_____

_____

_____

_____

_____

_____

_____

_____

_____

Date:	Starting From:	Companions
	Destination:	
Weather: ☀ ⛅ 🌧 🌨	Towns and Cities Explored:	Towns and Cities Explored:

Today's Travel Reflections:

_____

_____

_____

_____

_____

_____

_____

_____

_____

_____

_____

_____

_____

_____

_____

_____

_____

N

W   E

S

Sites Visited:

_____

_____

_____

_____

_____

_____

_____

_____

_____

I Will Never Forget:

_____

_____

_____

_____

_____

_____

_____

_____

_____

Date:	Starting From:	Companions
	Destination:	
Weather: ☀ ⛅ 🌧 🌨	Towns and Cities Explored:	Towns and Cities Explored:

Today's Travel Reflections:

_____

_____

_____

_____

_____

_____

_____

_____

_____

_____

_____

_____

_____

_____

_____

_____

Sites Visited:

_____
_____
_____
_____
_____
_____
_____
_____
_____

I Will Never Forget:

_____
_____
_____
_____
_____
_____
_____
_____
_____

Date:	Starting From:	Companions
	Destination:	
Weather: ☀ ⛅ 🌧 🌨	Towns and Cities Explored:	Towns and Cities Explored:

Today's Travel Reflections:

_____

_____

_____

_____

_____

_____

_____

_____

_____

_____

_____

_____

_____

_____

_____

_____

_____

_____

Sites Visited:

_____

_____

_____

_____

_____

_____

_____

_____

_____

_____

I Will Never Forget:

_____

_____

_____

_____

_____

_____

_____

_____

_____

Date:	Starting From:	Companions
	Destination:	
Weather: ☀ ⛅ 🌧 🌨	Towns and Cities Explored:	Towns and Cities Explored:

Today's Travel Reflections:

_____

_____

_____

_____

_____

_____

_____

_____

_____

_____

_____

_____

_____

_____

_____

_____

_____

Sites Visited:

_____

_____

_____

_____

_____

_____

_____

_____

_____

_____

I Will Never Forget:

_____

_____

_____

_____

_____

_____

_____

_____

_____

Date:	Starting From:	Companions
	Destination:	
Weather: ☀ ⛅ 🌧 🌨	Towns and Cities Explored:	Towns and Cities Explored:

Today's Travel Reflections:

_____

_____

_____

_____

_____

_____

_____

_____

_____

_____

_____

_____

_____

_____

_____

_____

_____

Sites Visited:

_____

_____

_____

_____

_____

_____

_____

_____

_____

_____

I Will Never Forget:

_____

_____

_____

_____

_____

_____

_____

_____

_____

Date:	Starting From:	Companions
	Destination:	
Weather: ☀ ⛅ 🌧 🌨	Towns and Cities Explored:	Towns and Cities Explored:

Today's Travel Reflections:

_____

_____

_____

_____

_____

_____

_____

_____

_____

_____

_____

_____

_____

_____

_____

_____

_____

Sites Visited:

_____

_____

_____

_____

_____

_____

_____

_____

_____

I Will Never Forget:

_____

_____

_____

_____

_____

_____

_____

_____

_____

Date:	Starting From: Destination:	Companions
Weather: ☀ ⛅ 🌧 🌨	Towns and Cities Explored:	Towns and Cities Explored:

Today's Travel Reflections:

_____

_____

_____

_____

_____

_____

_____

_____

_____

_____

_____

_____

_____

_____

_____

_____

Sites Visited:

_____

_____

_____

_____

_____

_____

_____

_____

_____

I Will Never Forget:

_____

_____

_____

_____

_____

_____

_____

_____

_____

Date:	Starting From: Destination:	Companions
Weather: ☀ ⛅ 🌧 🌨	Towns and Cities Explored:	Towns and Cities Explored:

Today's Travel Reflections:

_____

_____

_____

_____

_____

_____

_____

_____

_____

_____

_____

_____

_____

_____

_____

_____

_____

Sites Visited:

_____

_____

_____

_____

_____

_____

_____

_____

_____

_____

I Will Never Forget:

_____

_____

_____

_____

_____

_____

_____

_____

Date:	Starting From:	Companions
	Destination:	
Weather: ☀ ⛅ 🌧 🌨	Towns and Cities Explored:	Towns and Cities Explored:

Today's Travel Reflections:

_____

_____

_____

_____

_____

_____

_____

_____

_____

_____

_____

_____

_____

_____

_____

_____

_____

_____

Sites Visited:

_____

_____

_____

_____

_____

_____

_____

_____

_____

_____

I Will Never Forget:

_____

_____

_____

_____

_____

_____

_____

_____

_____

_____

Date:	Starting From:	Companions
	Destination:	
Weather: ☀ ⛅ 🌧 🌨	Towns and Cities Explored:	Towns and Cities Explored:

Today's Travel Reflections:

_____

_____

_____

_____

_____

_____

_____

_____

_____

_____

_____

_____

_____

_____

_____

_____

_____

Sites Visited:

_____

_____

_____

_____

_____

_____

_____

_____

I Will Never Forget:

_____

_____

_____

_____

_____

_____

_____

_____

Date:	Starting From:	Companions
	Destination:	
Weather: ☀ ⛅ 🌧 🌨	Towns and Cities Explored:	Towns and Cities Explored:

Today's Travel Reflections:

_____

_____

_____

_____

_____

_____

_____

_____

_____

_____

_____

_____

_____

_____

_____

_____

_____

_____

_____

Sites Visited:

_____

_____

_____

_____

_____

_____

_____

_____

_____

I Will Never Forget:

_____

_____

_____

_____

_____

_____

_____

_____

_____

Date:	Starting From:	Companions
	Destination:	
Weather: ☀ ⛅ 🌧 🌨	Towns and Cities Explored:	Towns and Cities Explored:

Today's Travel Reflections:

_____

_____

_____

_____

_____

_____

_____

_____

_____

_____

_____

_____

_____

_____

_____

_____

_____

Sites Visited:

_____

_____

_____

_____

_____

_____

_____

_____

_____

_____

I Will Never Forget:

_____

_____

_____

_____

_____

_____

_____

_____

_____

_____

Date:	Starting From:	Companions
	Destination:	
Weather: ☀ ⛅ 🌧 🌨	Towns and Cities Explored:	Towns and Cities Explored:

Today's Travel Reflections:

_____

_____

_____

_____

_____

_____

_____

_____

_____

_____

_____

_____

_____

_____

_____

_____

_____

Sites Visited:

_____

_____

_____

_____

_____

_____

_____

_____

_____

_____

I Will Never Forget:

_____

_____

_____

_____

_____

_____

_____

_____

_____

_____

Date:	Starting From:	Companions
	Destination:	
Weather: ☀ ⛅ 🌧 🌨	Towns and Cities Explored:	Towns and Cities Explored:

Today's Travel Reflections:

_____

_____

_____

_____

_____

_____

_____

_____

_____

_____

_____

_____

_____

_____

_____

_____

_____

Sites Visited:

_____

_____

_____

_____

_____

_____

_____

_____

_____

_____

I Will Never Forget:

_____

_____

_____

_____

_____

_____

_____

_____

_____

Date:	Starting From:	Companions
	Destination:	
Weather: ☀ ⛅ 🌧 🌨	Towns and Cities Explored:	Towns and Cities Explored:

Today's Travel Reflections:

_____

_____

_____

_____

_____

_____

_____

_____

_____

_____

_____

_____

_____

_____

_____

_____

_____

Sites Visited:

_____

_____

_____

_____

_____

_____

_____

_____

_____

I Will Never Forget:

_____

_____

_____

_____

_____

_____

_____

_____

_____

Date:	Starting From:	Companions
	Destination:	
Weather: ☀ ⛅ 🌧 🌨	Towns and Cities Explored:	Towns and Cities Explored:

Today's Travel Reflections:

_____

_____

_____

_____

_____

_____

_____

_____

_____

_____

_____

_____

_____

_____

_____

_____

_____

Sites Visited:

_____

_____

_____

_____

_____

_____

_____

_____

_____

_____

I Will Never Forget:

_____

_____

_____

_____

_____

_____

_____

_____

_____

Date:	Starting From:	Companions
	Destination:	
Weather: ☀ ⛅ 🌧 🌨	Towns and Cities Explored:	Towns and Cities Explored:

Today's Travel Reflections:

_____

_____

_____

_____

_____

_____

_____

_____

_____

_____

_____

_____

_____

_____

_____

_____

_____

Sites Visited:

_____

_____

_____

_____

_____

_____

_____

_____

_____

_____

I Will Never Forget:

_____

_____

_____

_____

_____

_____

_____

_____

_____

_____

Date:	Starting From:	Companions
	Destination:	
Weather: ☀ ⛅ 🌧 🌨	Towns and Cities Explored:	Towns and Cities Explored:

Today's Travel Reflections:

_____

_____

_____

_____

_____

_____

_____

_____

_____

_____

_____

_____

_____

_____

_____

Sites Visited:

_____

_____

_____

_____

_____

_____

_____

_____

_____

_____

I Will Never Forget:

_____

_____

_____

_____

_____

_____

_____

_____

_____

Date:	Starting From:	Companions
	Destination:	
Weather: ☀ ⛅ 🌧 🌨	Towns and Cities Explored:	Towns and Cities Explored:

Today's Travel Reflections:

_____

_____

_____

_____

_____

_____

_____

_____

_____

_____

_____

_____

_____

_____

_____

_____

_____

Sites Visited:

_____

_____

_____

_____

_____

_____

_____

_____

_____

I Will Never Forget:

_____

_____

_____

_____

_____

_____

_____

_____

_____

Date:	Starting From:	Companions
	Destination:	
Weather: ☀ ⛅ 🌧 🌨	Towns and Cities Explored:	Towns and Cities Explored:

Today's Travel Reflections:

_____

_____

_____

_____

_____

_____

_____

_____

_____

_____

_____

_____

_____

_____

_____

_____

Sites Visited:

_____

_____

_____

_____

_____

_____

_____

_____

_____

_____

I Will Never Forget:

_____

_____

_____

_____

_____

_____

_____

_____

_____

Date:	Starting From:	Companions
	Destination:	
Weather: ☼ ⛅ 🌧 🌨	Towns and Cities Explored:	Towns and Cities Explored:

Today's Travel Reflections:

_____

_____

_____

_____

_____

_____

_____

_____

_____

_____

_____

_____

_____

_____

_____

_____

Sites Visited:

_____

_____

_____

_____

_____

_____

_____

_____

_____

_____

I Will Never Forget:

_____

_____

_____

_____

_____

_____

_____

_____

_____

Date:	Starting From:	Companions
	Destination:	
Weather: ☀ ⛅ 🌧 🌨	Towns and Cities Explored:	Towns and Cities Explored:

Today's Travel Reflections:

_____

_____

_____

_____

_____

_____

_____

_____

_____

_____

_____

_____

_____

_____

_____

_____

_____

Sites Visited:

_____

_____

_____

_____

_____

_____

_____

_____

_____

_____

I Will Never Forget:

_____

_____

_____

_____

_____

_____

_____

_____

_____

_____

Date:	Starting From:	Companions
	Destination:	
Weather: ☀ ⛅ 🌧 🌨	Towns and Cities Explored:	Towns and Cities Explored:

Today's Travel Reflections:

_____

_____

_____

_____

_____

_____

_____

_____

_____

_____

_____

_____

_____

_____

_____

_____

Sites Visited:

_____

_____

_____

_____

_____

_____

_____

_____

_____

_____

I Will Never Forget:

_____

_____

_____

_____

_____

_____

_____

_____

_____

Date:	Starting From:	Companions
	Destination:	
Weather: ☀ ⛅ 🌧 🌨	Towns and Cities Explored:	Towns and Cities Explored:

Today's Travel Reflections:

_____

_____

_____

_____

_____

_____

_____

_____

_____

_____

_____

_____

_____

_____

_____

_____

_____

Sites Visited:

_____

_____

_____

_____

_____

_____

_____

_____

_____

I Will Never Forget:

_____

_____

_____

_____

_____

_____

_____

_____

_____

Date:	Starting From:	Companions
	Destination:	
Weather: ☀ ⛅ 🌧 🌨	Towns and Cities Explored:	Towns and Cities Explored:

Today's Travel Reflections:

_____

_____

_____

_____

_____

_____

_____

_____

_____

_____

_____

_____

_____

_____

_____

_____

_____

Sites Visited:

_____
_____
_____
_____
_____
_____
_____
_____
_____
_____
_____

I Will Never Forget:

_____
_____
_____
_____
_____
_____
_____
_____
_____
_____
_____

Date:	Starting From:	Companions
	Destination:	
Weather: ☀ ⛅ 🌧 🌨	Towns and Cities Explored:	Towns and Cities Explored:

Today's Travel Reflections:

_____

_____

_____

_____

_____

_____

_____

_____

_____

_____

_____

_____

_____

_____

_____

_____

_____

Sites Visited:

_____

_____

_____

_____

_____

_____

_____

_____

_____

I Will Never Forget:

_____

_____

_____

_____

_____

_____

_____

_____

_____

Date:	Starting From:	Companions
	Destination:	
Weather: ☀ ⛅ 🌧 🌨	Towns and Cities Explored:	Towns and Cities Explored:

Today's Travel Reflections:

_____

_____

_____

_____

_____

_____

_____

_____

_____

_____

_____

_____

_____

_____

_____

_____

Sites Visited:

_____

_____

_____

_____

_____

_____

_____

_____

_____

_____

I Will Never Forget:

_____

_____

_____

_____

_____

_____

_____

_____

_____

Date:	Starting From:	Companions
	Destination:	
Weather: ☀ ⛅ 🌧 🌨	Towns and Cities Explored:	Towns and Cities Explored:

Today's Travel Reflections:

_____

_____

_____

_____

_____

_____

_____

_____

_____

_____

_____

_____

_____

_____

_____

_____

_____

Sites Visited:

_____

_____

_____

_____

_____

_____

_____

_____

_____

_____

I Will Never Forget:

_____

_____

_____

_____

_____

_____

_____

_____

_____

Date:	Starting From:	Companions
	Destination:	
Weather: ☀ ⛅ 🌧 🌨	Towns and Cities Explored:	Towns and Cities Explored:

Today's Travel Reflections:

_____

_____

_____

_____

_____

_____

_____

_____

_____

_____

_____

_____

_____

_____

_____

Sites Visited:

_____

_____

_____

_____

_____

_____

_____

_____

_____

_____

I Will Never Forget:

_____

_____

_____

_____

_____

_____

_____

_____

_____

_____

Date:	Starting From:	Companions
	Destination:	
Weather: ☀ ⛅ 🌧 🌨	Towns and Cities Explored:	Towns and Cities Explored:

Today's Travel Reflections:

_____

_____

_____

_____

_____

_____

_____

_____

_____

_____

_____

_____

_____

_____

_____

Sites Visited:

_____

_____

_____

_____

_____

_____

_____

_____

_____

_____

I Will Never Forget:

_____

_____

_____

_____

_____

_____

_____

_____

_____

_____

Date:	Starting From:	Companions
	Destination:	
Weather: ☀ ⛅ 🌧 🌨	Towns and Cities Explored:	Towns and Cities Explored:

Today's Travel Reflections:

_____

_____

_____

_____

_____

_____

_____

_____

_____

_____

_____

_____

_____

_____

_____

Sites Visited:

_____

_____

_____

_____

_____

_____

_____

_____

_____

_____

I Will Never Forget:

_____

_____

_____

_____

_____

_____

_____

_____

_____

_____

Date:	Starting From:	Companions
	Destination:	
Weather: ☀ ⛅ 🌧 🌨	Towns and Cities Explored:	Towns and Cities Explored:

Today's Travel Reflections:

_____

_____

_____

_____

_____

_____

_____

_____

_____

_____

_____

_____

_____

_____

_____

_____

_____

Sites Visited:

_____

_____

_____

_____

_____

_____

_____

_____

_____

_____

I Will Never Forget:

_____

_____

_____

_____

_____

_____

_____

_____

_____

_____

Date:	Starting From:	Companions
	Destination:	
Weather: ☀ ⛅ 🌧 🌨	Towns and Cities Explored:	Towns and Cities Explored:

Today's Travel Reflections:

_____

_____

_____

_____

_____

_____

_____

_____

_____

_____

_____

_____

_____

_____

_____

_____

_____

_____

Sites Visited:

_____

_____

_____

_____

_____

_____

_____

_____

_____

_____

I Will Never Forget:

_____

_____

_____

_____

_____

_____

_____

_____

_____

Date:	Starting From:	Companions
	Destination:	
Weather: ☀ ⛅ 🌧 🌨	Towns and Cities Explored:	Towns and Cities Explored:

Today's Travel Reflections:

_____

_____

_____

_____

_____

_____

_____

_____

_____

_____

_____

_____

_____

_____

Sites Visited:

_____

_____

_____

_____

_____

_____

_____

_____

_____

_____

I Will Never Forget:

_____

_____

_____

_____

_____

_____

_____

_____

_____

_____

Date:	Starting From:	Companions
	Destination:	
Weather: ☀ ⛅ 🌧 🌨	Towns and Cities Explored:	Towns and Cities Explored:

Today's Travel Reflections:

_____

_____

_____

_____

_____

_____

_____

_____

_____

_____

_____

_____

_____

_____

_____

_____

Sites Visited:

_____

_____

_____

_____

_____

_____

_____

_____

_____

I Will Never Forget:

_____

_____

_____

_____

_____

_____

_____

_____

_____

Date:	Starting From:	Companions
	Destination:	
Weather: ☀ ⛅ 🌧 🌨	Towns and Cities Explored:	Towns and Cities Explored:

Today's Travel Reflections:

_____

_____

_____

_____

_____

_____

_____

_____

_____

_____

_____

_____

_____

_____

_____

_____

_____

Sites Visited:

_____

_____

_____

_____

_____

_____

_____

_____

_____

_____

_____

I Will Never Forget:

_____

_____

_____

_____

_____

_____

_____

_____

_____

_____

Date:	Starting From:	Companions
	Destination:	
Weather: ☀ ⛅ 🌧 🌨	Towns and Cities Explored:	Towns and Cities Explored:

Today's Travel Reflections:

_____

_____

_____

_____

_____

_____

_____

_____

_____

_____

_____

_____

_____

_____

_____

_____

_____

Sites Visited:

_____

_____

_____

_____

_____

_____

_____

_____

I Will Never Forget:

_____

_____

_____

_____

_____

_____

_____

_____

If you enjoyed this journal, we have many more styles and types to choose from. Visit our website for a complete list of journals.

www.wanderingwalksofwonder.com

National Parks Journal

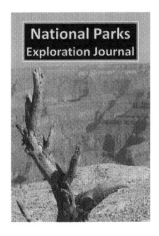

Bucket List Journal

Kid's Travel Journal

Lighthouse Exploration Journal

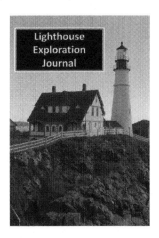

44197787R00050

Made in the USA
Middletown, DE
31 May 2017